Twiggy Winkles

NEWTON ABBOT 01626 62319

ELIZABETH DYAS

Illustrations by **Guy Dyas**
Photographs by **'Flair' and Chris Wormald**

ISBN. 1 898964 13 0

Published by Orchard Publications, 2 Orchard Close, Chudleigh. TQ13 0LR Tel. (01626) 852714
Designed, Typeset and Printed by Swiftprint, Dawlish, Devon. EX7 9HP

In the beginning … Twiggy Winkies opened as a small mixed farm *(to the public)* in 1990. Throughout the first year people brought hedgehogs in boxes, injured or ill for us to treat, we did not know anything about hedgehogs and kept sending them away! But they kept coming much to our embarrassment! At the end of the season the British Hedgehog Preservation Society came to our aid. After a winter attending seminars and teach ins, we approached the next season with a little more confidence. After a very hectic season we realised that the 10ft by 10ft hospital was much too small, how we coped with so many patients we will never know!

Since those early days the hospital has grown and so has our knowledge and care - with new techniques, better equipment and medications we are able to care for hundreds of hedgehogs admitted from the RSPCA and kindly members of the public.

During the summer months with hundreds of holiday makers and local families visiting the farm to enjoy the farm activities, it is a major exercise for us to organise the frequent bottle feeding of farm babies and the 2 hourly feeds required by baby hogs who need feeding through the night as well!

If you see a baby hog, please just observe at a distance, do not handle, the mother will probably return and if it has been touched she will reject it. However if you are sure the mother will not return, or the baby is injured, keep the baby warm and contact the RSPCA as soon as possible for advice and help. They will find a local registered carer or will advise about the care and feeding *(they will also treat any injury or illness)*. Cows milk is not good for hedgehogs and may actually kill the babies.

The hedgehog is Britain's only spiny mammal, a delightful wild animal as well as the gardener's friend.

Hedgehogs are mainly meat eaters but they also eat all other sorts of food. As well as beetles, worms and slugs, they enjoy bananas, nuts, and cereal along with bread and biscuit.

They can be found in parks, gardens and farmland and they prefer hedgerows and areas of uncultivated land where there are plenty of insects and materials and cover to make a nest.

Today with our neat gardens, use of labour saving machinery and pesticides, and farmers removing their hedgerows, the habitat is vanishing and the number of hedgehogs will also diminish.

Surely it is up to all of us to see that our wild animals are there for our children and grandchildren to enjoy.

Hedgehogs start to wake up when the warmer weather arrives usually around April or May, they need to eat plenty of food to put on the weight they have lost during the long winter months, even though they may have had an odd small meal during warmer spells during the winter.

Courtship is a long and very noisy affair, much snorting and snuffling and moving round each other in circles. After mating the male disappears leaving the female to carry, give birth and care for the young.

Most babies are born in June and July but can be born as late as October. Pregnancy lasts 34 days. The average litter size is 4 - 6 young, born in a well constructed nest of leaves, grass and often paper or old rags left lying about, and placed under a pile of logs or an old garden shed.

Man has created so many hazards for hedgehogs. Vehicles kill thousands on the roads every year, their habitat is destroyed by gardeners and farmers, cattle grids and ponds are constructed without an escape ramp. Machinery and chemicals are used indiscriminately, and tins and yoghurt pots are left lying about for them to get trapped inside. Even nets and wire netting become a danger when their prickles become entangled in them. Let us all make an effort to look after our own area to make it a safer place for all wild animals.

Hedgehog Menu

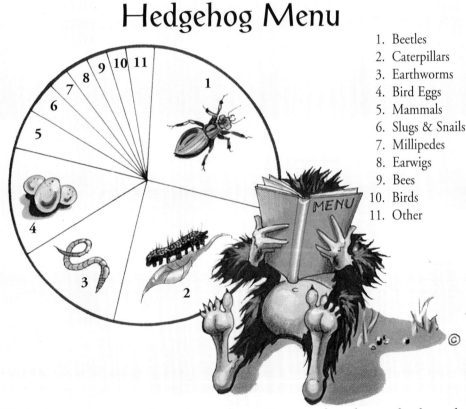

1. Beetles
2. Caterpillars
3. Earthworms
4. Bird Eggs
5. Mammals
6. Slugs & Snails
7. Millipedes
8. Earwigs
9. Bees
10. Birds
11. Other

Hedgehogs do sometimes have fleas! Do not be alarmed, they do not live on humans or other animals, a sprinkle of Johnson's Baby Bird powder will remove them. Occasionally a tick may be present but will drop off if covered in any kind of oil after about 48 hours. If maggots are present it usually indicates that there is an open wound and need to be removed with tweezers as soon as possible.

CARE OF
Baby Hedgehogs

Baby hogs under about 8 weeks old need specialised care and are better handed to the RSPCA or a registered carer experienced in this field. They need constant warmth, special milk with added colostrum and vitamins, and very careful handling. Even with special care many will not survive. At Twiggy Winkies we have experienced staff and equipment to care for the babies.

The Hedgehog Year

Waking
Up

Courtship

Mother
with
Babies

Mother and young leave the nest

Young and independent

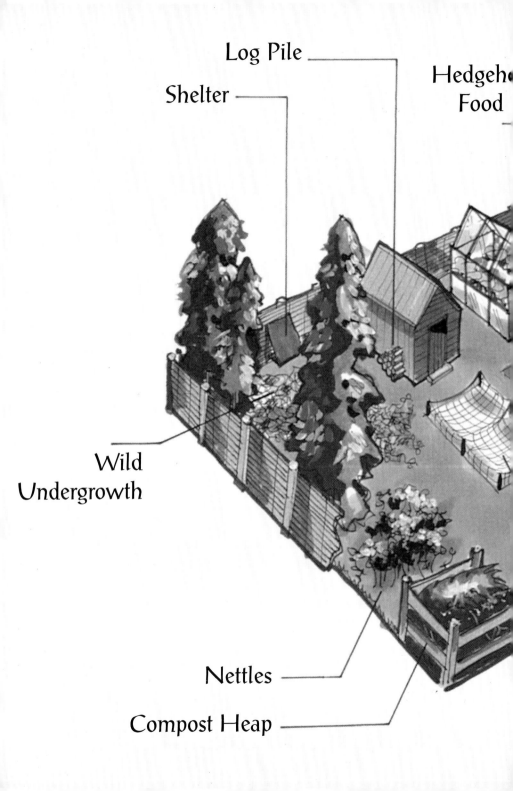

Log Pile

Shelter

Hedgeh⋯
Food

Wild
Undergrowth

Nettles

Compost Heap

A Hedgehog - Friendly Garden

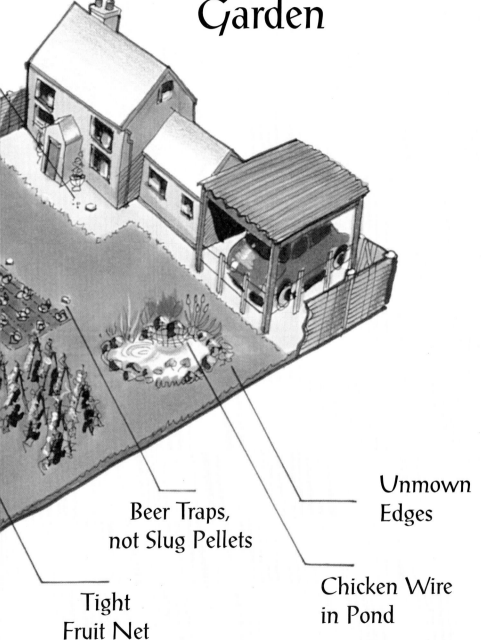

Beer Traps,
not Slug Pellets

Unmown
Edges

Tight
Fruit Net

Chicken Wire
in Pond

Hibernation

When the weather gets colder and food is more difficult to find, hedgehogs will look for a place to build a winter nest, in Britain this is usually from November to April. The hedgehog collects dry leaves and grasses and carries them to a suitably protected site, under a pile of wood or a garden shed. Once inside they shuffle round and round to make the nest cosy and waterproof. In hibernation the body temperature may fall to as low as 34° F, the pulse rate may be 20 beats per minute and respiration once every few minutes.

Collecting bedding for hibernation

Hibernating

The Importance of Weighing In.

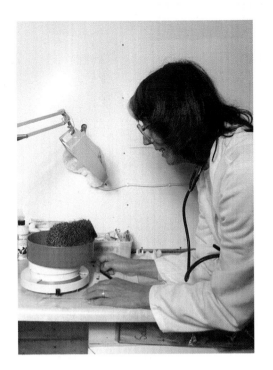

Autumn Babies

Many baby hogs born late in the season may fail to survive. They need to weigh at least 1lb by October to survive hibernation, below this weight, unless taken indoors and fed, they will surely die. Every year kindly animal carers give shelter and food to under-weight hedgehogs, keeping them through the long winter months and then releasing them on a fine spring day.

©

Day old babies in the incubator.

Baby hogs at 14 days old, their eyes are just open.

Youngsters tuck into a meaty meal.

Newly born baby hogs are pink and bald, but soon after birth pure white prickles grow through the grey skin on the back. They are blind and deaf, very mobile and have a high pitched squeak when they are hungry. Length varies from 2 - 4 inches at birth and weight about 2 - 6 ozs. The babies need constant warmth and they need to feed from the mother hedgehog often. Unlike other mammals baby hedgehogs need colostrum for six weeks after birth. Colostrum is the first milk produced by lactating mammals, the milk is rich in antibodies to help protect the baby from infections.

By the time they are 36 hours old, dark brown prickles with white tips grow and by the time they are one week old, and still blind and deaf the skin takes on a grey look and there may be a few small whiskers by the nose. The eyes and ears open anytime between 12 - 20 days.

A hedgehog aged three weeks will have a good set of prickles with very few of the original white ones, and the rest of the body and legs have a covering of soft brown fur. The nose is blunt in shape and the first teeth appear.

At four weeks old the babies look like miniature adults and the mother will take the young with her to teach them to forage for food.

At eight weeks old and weighing 12ozs or more they are ready to leave the nest.

From Birth to 4 Weeks

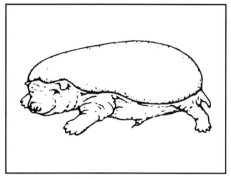

Hedgehog at Birth

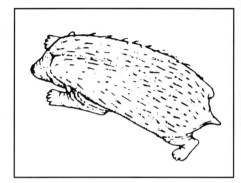

1 Hour Old

36 Hours Old

One Week Old

Three Weeks Old

Four Weeks Old

Baby Feeding

Cleaning a baby hog

When releasing hedgehogs back into the wild choose a place away from roads with trees and hedgerows, and where there are known to be other hedgehogs. Badgers enjoy hedgehogs for a meal so check that the area is not in a territory of badgers. It is a good idea to give the hedgehog some time in an outdoor pen to get him used to the change of temperature, and to provide his natural diet at dusk. On a warm evening release him near some undergrowth. In case he returns put some water and catfood out for him over the next few evenings.

If you are releasing hedgehogs in late autumn, they should weigh at least 400gms to stand a chance of survival. They do not store a supply of food to last through the winter, they rely on fat stored below the skin, so hedgehogs eat plenty before hibernation to build up a fatty layer to last through the winter months.

Acknowledgements ...

THE **RSPCA**
THE BRITISH HEDGEHOG PRESERVATION SOCIETY
THE MAMMAL SOCIETY
THE WELSH HEDGEHOG HOSPITAL
THE BRITISH WILDLIFE REHABILITATION COUNCIL

There is a country wide 24 hr emergency telephone number for the RSPCA

01345 888999

Diana with Tyler and Ben

ISBN. 1 898964 13 0